Ladybird

OCEAN

CONTENTS

OCEANS AND SEAS

One huge body of salt water surrounds the islands and continents of Earth, covering nearly three-quarters of the planet. The four largest areas of water are called oceans: the Atlantic, Pacific, Indian, and Arctic. Smaller areas are called seas. They include the Red, Baltic, Mediterranean, and Caribbean, among others.

The Salty Seas

Rocks in riverbeds contain sodium. Water rushing over the rocks gradually dissolves them and carries the sodium to the seas and oceans, making them salty. Gold, silver, and other **minerals** are also found in sea water.

CURRENTS, WAVES, AND TIDES

Ocean water is always in motion. This constant ebb and flow of the sea is caused by currents, waves, and tides.

Currents

Currents are continual movements of air and water around the globe. Air currents create currents in the water by constantly pushing on its surface. These ocean currents move cold water from the North and South Poles towards the equator, where the water warms up and then circles back toward the poles. This constant motion keeps ocean temperatures from varying drastically. Even so, the waters at the poles are near freezing, while those at the equator are like a warm bath.

The fastest current in the world is the Agulhas Current, which flows along the west coast of Africa. It moves at a speed of about five miles per hour.

Waves

Wind blowing on the surface of the sea causes **waves**. The stronger the wind and water current, the bigger the waves. When a wave hits a beach, it breaks, or curls, and the water drains back into the ocean.

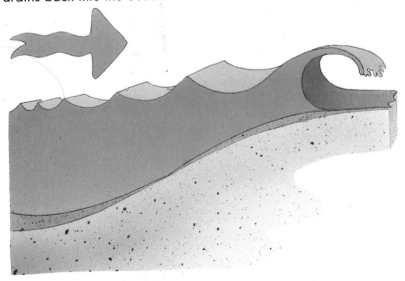

Tides

Twice a day, every day, the ocean gradually moves up the shore and back down again. These movements are called **tides**.

You can spot the high-tide mark by looking for seaweed and other debris from the sea high up on the beach.

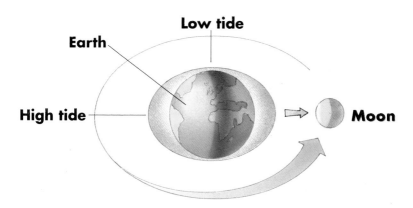

Low tide

Earth

High tide

Moon

Tides are the result of the daily pull of the moon's **gravity** on the ocean. Tide levels vary each day and in different parts of the world. About once every two weeks, when the moon and sun are aligned with Earth, the gravitational pull becomes stronger, making high tides higher and low tides lower. These are called spring tides.

SAVING THE SEAS

The oceans are home to a vast array of plant and animal life. **Pollution**, however, has built up in these great bodies of water, threatening many aquatic species. For years, trash, chemical waste, and other pollutants were dumped into the oceans. Today, in many parts of the world, it is illegal for businesses to dump waste into the water.

Danger from Sewage
Releasing raw **sewage** into the sea is dangerous because harmful bacteria can survive in water.

Hazards from Ships
Oil spills from damaged tankers kill marine life and sea birds.

Garbage
Trash thrown from ships entangles and kills wildlife.

Overfishing is another threat to sea life. Many fish are **endangered** because too many are caught before they have time to reproduce. Steps are being taken to protect our marine environment. Limits placed on the number of fish taken with nets will help reduce overfishing.

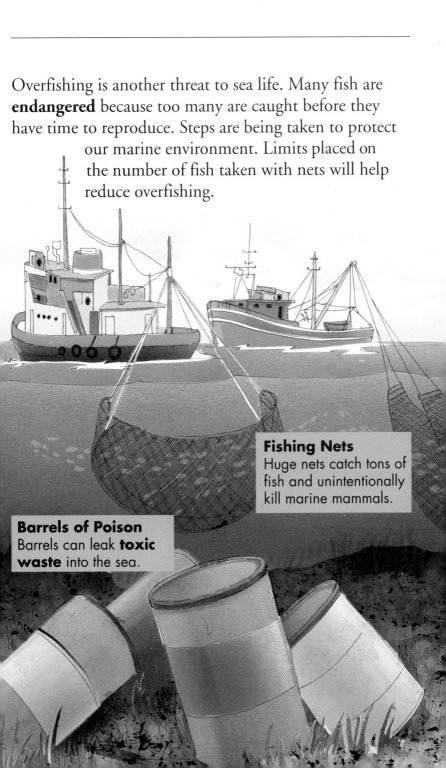

Fishing Nets
Huge nets catch tons of fish and unintentionally kill marine mammals.

Barrels of Poison
Barrels can leak **toxic waste** into the sea.

ALONG THE SEASHORE

Not all seashores look alike. Some are muddy; others are covered with rocks or sand. Sand is made from rocks and shells that have been broken up into very fine particles by the sea. Sand comes in various colors, depending on the kind of rock it is from. Coral sand is white and pink. Quartz becomes yellow sand; volcanic rock makes black sand.

In some areas, waves crash against cliffs instead of sandy beaches. The water slowly wears away the cliffs, carving out arches and caves.

Birds
At low tide, wading birds look for food in **tide pools**.

Curlews
These birds use their long, pointed beaks to probe the sand in search of worms.

Seashore Life

Animals and plants living along the seashore and in tide pools have adapted to the rise and fall of tides. Limpets cling tightly to the rocks so that they are not swept out to sea. Root-like anchors help seaweeds hold on to rocks. A coating of slime keeps the plants from drying out during low tide.

Barnacles

Mussels

Sea Anemone

Starfish

Limpets

Shrimp

Crab

Bladder Wrack

THE OCEAN FLOOR

Like the surface of Earth, the ocean floor consists of deep valleys, flat plains, active volcanoes, and high mountains. The tops of some underwater mountains rise above the surface of the water, forming islands.

Deep-Sea Trenches

Around the edges of the Pacific Ocean are deep **trenches** in Earth's oceanic crust. Down over 36,000 feet, the deepest point in the planet's oceans is located in the Pacific, at the bottom of the Mariana Trench.

Deep-Sea Mountains
Running from pole to pole, the Mid-Atlantic Ridge is the longest mountain range in the world.

Seamounts, isolated underwater mountains, rise up from the ocean floor. One of the biggest is the Great Meteor Seamount in the Atlantic Ocean, which is 13,000 feet high.

Abyssal Plains are flat areas deep below the surface of the sea. They make up about half the ocean floor.

OCEAN FISH

Fish have adapted to life in all the world's oceans. In the Antarctic Ocean, for example, ice fish have developed special chemicals in their blood that help them keep from freezing.

Flying Fish
These fish can leap out of the water to escape danger.

Cod
Cod live in **schools** close to the surface. When breeding, they scatter their eggs in the sea.

Sharks
Sharks are the most feared fish in the sea. But not all sharks are dangerous.

Flatfish
A newly hatched flatfish is shaped like other fish. But as it grows older, one of its eyes moves to the other side of its body, next to its other eye. The flatfish swims close to the ocean floor, using the fins along the edge of its body.

Deep below the surface of the ocean, the water is inky black and icy cold. It is also heavy enough to crush a human being! Despite such conditions, all kinds of unusual creatures live in the deepest, darkest parts of the sea.

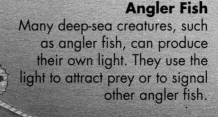

Angler Fish
Many deep-sea creatures, such as angler fish, can produce their own light. They use the light to attract prey or to signal other angler fish.

Gulper Eel
The huge mouth and flexible stomach of the gulper eel allow it to swallow whole fish.

Tripod Fish
These fish balance above the sea floor, supported on three thin fins, just like a camera on a tripod. When prey passes by, tripod fish quickly pounce.

MARINE REPTILES

Marine reptiles live mainly in the tropical seas, where the water is warm and they can maintain their body temperatures. In colder waters, reptiles' bodies cool down and they become less active. There are fewer than sixty species of marine reptiles alive today, but hundreds of ancient species have been preserved as **fossils**.

Leatherback Turtle
Of the seven species of sea turtles, the leatherback is the largest. These turtles live in all of the world's oceans.

Sea Snake
There are about fifty different kinds of sea snakes. Some are brightly colored; all are highly poisonous. Sea snakes feed mainly on fish.

Sea Crocodile
Some crocodiles can live in both fresh and salt water. The saltwater crocodile of Southeast Asia can grow to be 30 feet long! At sea, crocodiles often relax and drift with the currents.

SEA BIRDS

Many birds live close to the coast and move inland in bad weather. Others nest and raise families on cliffs. A few birds, such as the albatross, spend long periods of time gliding over the oceans, far from land. When they get hungry, they drop down to scoop up fish from the sea.

Frigate Bird
The "pirate of the skies" steals its food from other birds. It forces them to drop their catch and then grabs the food before it falls into the sea.

Pelicans
The huge, expandable pouch under a pelican's beak acts as a fishing net. A pelican catches fish by moving its open mouth under the water. It then drains the water and swallows its catch.

Oystercatcher
This is one of the wading birds that live along the shoreline. The oystercatcher uses its blunt beak as a chisel to break shellfish off rocks.

17

PREHISTORIC SEA CREATURES

Fish were the first animals with backbones to evolve in the seas, nearly 500 million years ago. All fish, prehistoric and present-day, have gills—organs located behind the eyes that extract oxygen from the water. Fish do not need to come up to the surface to breathe. The animals on these two pages are extinct fish. The extinct reptiles, mammals, and sea birds on the next pages were air-breathers.

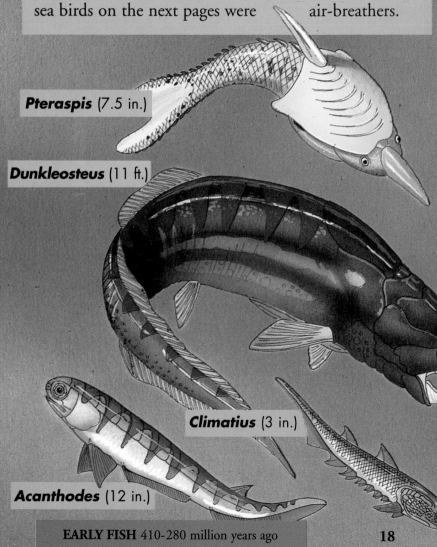

Pteraspis (7.5 in.)

Dunkleosteus (11 ft.)

Climatius (3 in.)

Acanthodes (12 in.)

EARLY FISH 410-280 million years ago

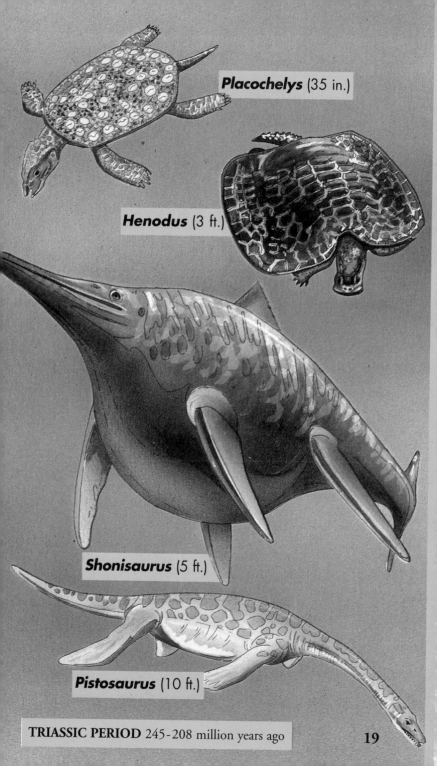

Placochelys (35 in.)

Henodus (3 ft.)

Shonisaurus (5 ft.)

Pistosaurus (10 ft.)

TRIASSIC PERIOD 245-208 million years ago

19

Herring

Mackerel

Cod

Sardine

Blue Shark

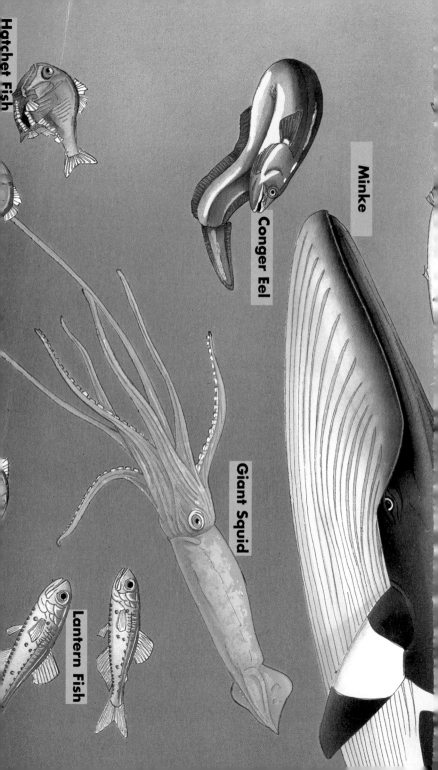

Hatchet Fish

Minke

Conger Eel

Giant Squid

Lantern Fish

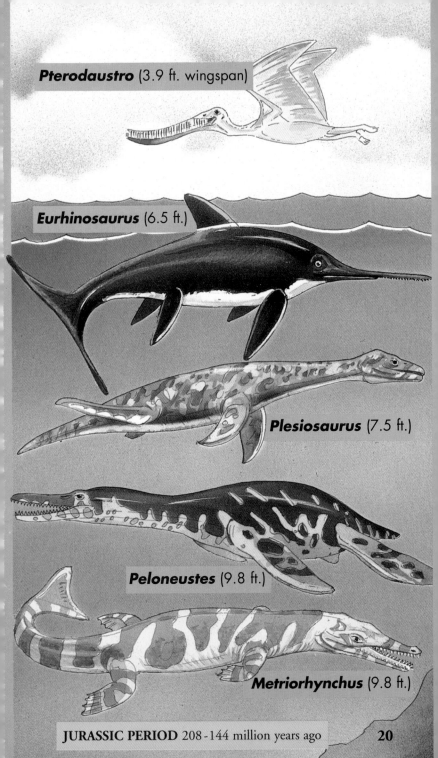

Pterodaustro (3.9 ft. wingspan)

Eurhinosaurus (6.5 ft.)

Plesiosaurus (7.5 ft.)

Peloneustes (9.8 ft.)

Metriorhynchus (9.8 ft.)

Osteodontornis orri (19.5 ft. wingspan)

Prorastomus (5 ft.)

Protocetus (8 ft.)

Eurhinodelphis (6.5 ft.)

Basilosaurus (82 ft.)

TERTIARY PERIOD 66-1.6 million years ago

21

THE DISCOVERY OF THE COELACANTH

In 1938, the crew of a fishing boat caught a fish unlike any they had ever seen before. An expert from the local museum identified the fish. It was a coelacanth—a fish thought to have been extinct for more than sixty million years! Today, collectors and souvenir hunters threaten to make the coelacanth extinct once and for all.

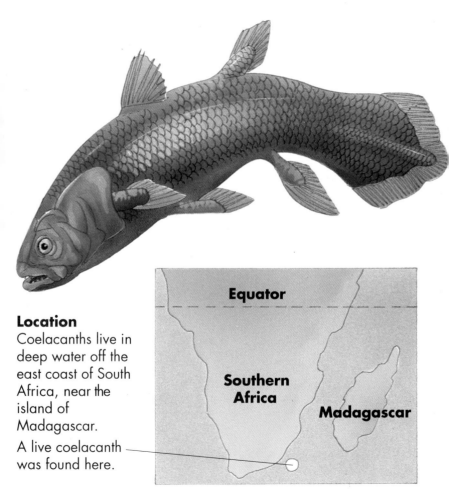

Location
Coelacanths live in deep water off the east coast of South Africa, near the island of Madagascar.

A live coelacanth was found here.

Equator

Southern Africa

Madagascar

SEA MAMMALS

Many different species of mammals live in the ocean. All sea mammals breathe air and give birth to live young. Some sea mammals, such as whales and dolphins, spend their whole lives in the water while others, such as seals and walruses, divide their time between land and sea.

Sea Otter
When the sea otter naps, it wraps itself in seaweed. The plants anchor the otter, to keep it from floating away. The sea otter also likes to sleep with its front paws over its eyes.

Sea Lion
Sea lions can swim faster than all other seals, reaching speeds of 25 miles per hour over short distances.

Whale
Whales can hold their breath for several hours underwater before coming up to the surface for air.

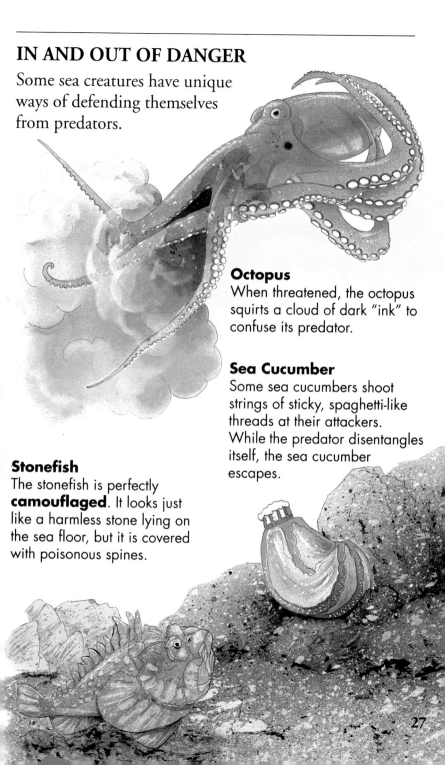

IN AND OUT OF DANGER

Some sea creatures have unique ways of defending themselves from predators.

Octopus
When threatened, the octopus squirts a cloud of dark "ink" to confuse its predator.

Sea Cucumber
Some sea cucumbers shoot strings of sticky, spaghetti-like threads at their attackers. While the predator disentangles itself, the sea cucumber escapes.

Stonefish
The stonefish is perfectly **camouflaged**. It looks just like a harmless stone lying on the sea floor, but it is covered with poisonous spines.

LIFE ON A CORAL REEF

Coral reefs grow in warm, shallow water in tropical seas. The coral is made up of millions of tiny sea creatures called coral **polyps**. The polyps build stony cases around their soft bodies for protection. When they die, the hard cases remain and gradually build up into a reef. One third of all fish make their homes among coral reefs.

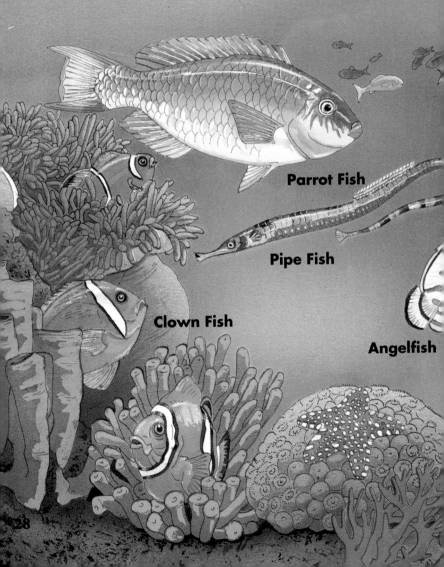

Parrot Fish

Pipe Fish

Clown Fish

Angelfish

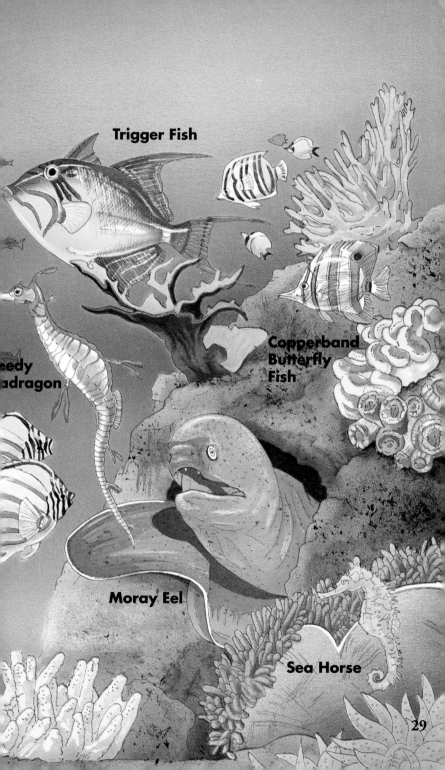

Trigger Fish

Copperband Butterfly Fish

eedy
adragon

Moray Eel

Sea Horse

SEA GIANTS AND DWARFS

Ocean life comes in all shapes and sizes, from the gigantic blue whale to tiny plants smaller than the head of a pin.

Blue Whale
The blue whale is the largest animal in the world. It can grow to be 100 feet long and weigh up to 150 tons.

Atlantic Giant Squid
This squid has the biggest eyes of any known animal. The largest squid ever found was washed ashore in Newfoundland in 1878. Its tentacles were 36 feet long.

Dwarf Goby
The smallest fish in the sea is the dwarf goby, which lives in the Indian Ocean. Fully grown, it is less than half an inch long.

Whale Shark

The biggest fish in the sea, the whale shark can be over 39 feet long and weigh over 13 tons. It feeds mainly on **zooplankton**. The whale shark is not dangerous to human swimmers.

Pacific Giant Kelp

A single strand of this seaweed can measure over 195 feet long, which makes it the largest plant in the sea.

Phytoplankton

These are the smallest sea plants, which can be seen only under a microscope. They drift on the surface of the water, providing food for many sea animals.

EXPLORING THE SEA

People have sailed the seas for thousands of years, in vessels that range from the simple dugout canoes of ancient cultures to the huge oil tankers used today. Early sailors relied on the sun, moon, and stars to help them **navigate**. Explorers looked for exotic land and people, while merchants searched for profitable new trade routes.

A Polynesian Raft

The Polynesian people of the South Pacific built canoes from hollowed-out tree trunks. Two canoes were lashed together to create a raft. Polynesian sailors used both sails and paddles to propel their boats.

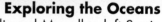

Exploring the Oceans

Ferdinand Magellan left Spain with five ships and 260 men in 1519, in search of a western route to the Spice Islands in the East Indies. Although the expedition eventually succeeded, Magellan was killed, and only one ship and 18 men survived. It was the first voyage around the world.

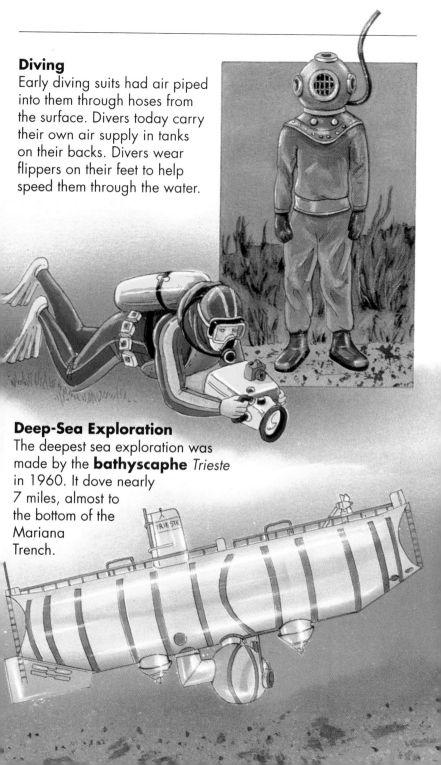

Diving

Early diving suits had air piped into them through hoses from the surface. Divers today carry their own air supply in tanks on their backs. Divers wear flippers on their feet to help speed them through the water.

Deep-Sea Exploration

The deepest sea exploration was made by the **bathyscaphe** *Trieste* in 1960. It dove nearly 7 miles, almost to the bottom of the Mariana Trench.

TREASURES FROM THE SEA

The sea contains some of Earth's most valuable natural resources. It holds a wealth of fish, plants, and animals that can be harvested for food. It is also rich in oil, gas, and minerals. Wells are drilled into the seabed, and oil or gas is pumped up to the surface.

Oil Rig

Drilling for oil and gas in the sea is expensive and dangerous. The rigs, or floating wells, are highly flammable. People have to stay and work on them, usually for two-week shifts. Helicopters transport workers to and from the rig.

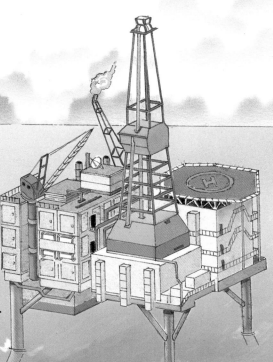

Treasure in a Shell

The life of a pearl begins when an oyster or clam gets a speck of sand inside its shell. The oyster covers the speck with layers of a chemical called calcium carbonate. The layers build up into a pearl.

Finding Treasure
Underwater archaeologists study sunken ships.

Ancient jars, coins, bars of gold, jewelry, and other treasures may still lie undiscovered on the ocean floor.

Underwater Exploration
Scientists use research submersibles to find shipwrecks, photograph them, and help retrieve artifacts from deep water.

AMAZING SEA FACTS

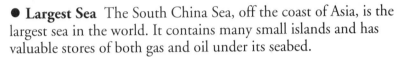
Sea Otter

● **Feeding Habits** To get the tasty food inside shellfish, the otter floats on its back, places a rock on its stomach, and then cracks the shell open.

● **Diving Birds** The emperor penguin of Antarctica can dive 820 feet below the surface of the sea.

● **Largest Sea** The South China Sea, off the coast of Asia, is the largest sea in the world. It contains many small islands and has valuable stores of both gas and oil under its seabed.

● **Clearest Water** The clearest sea water is in the Weddell Sea, close to Antarctica. From the surface, an object 11 inches wide can be seen 262 feet below the surface.

● **Greatest Number of Eggs** The female ocean sunfish can lay as many as 30 million eggs at one time.

● **Sea Bird Fertilizer** Huge pillars of bird droppings, some over 295 feet tall, have built up over thousands of years from colonies of sea birds nesting on islands off the coast of Peru. In the 1800s, people began destroying the columns and selling the droppings as a fertilizer, called "guano."

Sea Lion

● **Largest Ocean** The Pacific is the world's largest ocean. Excluding the seas surrounding it, the Pacific Ocean represents nearly 50 percent of the surface of Earth covered by water.

● **Getting Around** Sea lions turn their rear flippers forward to help support their bodies on land. They then walk on their front and back flippers. Seals that can't walk slide over land by contracting their strong stomach muscles.

GLOSSARY

Abyssal plain Large, flat area that forms the floor of the deep ocean, away from the edges of land.

Bathyscaphe An underwater craft used for exploring the deepest parts of the ocean.

Camouflage The way in which a creature hides itself, using its body shape or color to blend into its surroundings.

Current The route air or water takes as it moves around the globe.

Endangered When a species is in danger of dying out and disappearing from Earth.

Equator An imaginary line around the middle of Earth.

Extinct Vanished: the species no longer exists.

Fossil The remains or impression of an animal or plant that have been preserved in mud, sediment, or rock.

Gravity The force that pulls the sea toward the moon, creating tides.

Mineral A chemical that is present on land and may dissolve in water.

Navigate To direct or steer the course of a ship on a journey.

Pesticide A combination of chemicals used to kill pests that feed on crops.

Phytoplankton Microscopic oceanic plants that are a vital source of food for many sea creatures.

Poles The most northern and southern points on Earth.

Pollution Trash, chemical waste, and other materials that damage the environment.

Polyps Tiny creatures whose remains gradually build up into coral reefs.

School A group of the same fish swimming together.

Seamount An underwater mountain.

Sewage Human waste material.

Tide The gradual, daily movement of the sea up and down the beach.

Tide pool The rocky area that traps sea water when the tide goes out.

Toxic waste Poisonous chemical waste material.

Trench A crack or trough in the ocean floor.

Wave The surface movement of the sea, caused by winds.

Zooplankton Small crustaceans, tiny fish, and fish larvae.

INDEX *(Entries in **bold** refer to an illustration)*